The Piano Teacher

The Piano Teacher

A Healing Key

A PLAY BY

Dorothy Dittrich

Foreword by Yvette Nolan

Introduction by Rachel Ditor

TALONBOOKS

Talonbooks
9259 Shaughnessy Street, Vancouver, British Columbia, Canada V6P 6R4
talonbooks.com

Talonbooks is located on xʷməθkʷəy̓əm, Sḵwx̱wú7mesh, and səl̓ilwətaʔɬ Lands.

First printing: 2022

Typeset in Minion
Printed and bound in Canada on 100% post-consumer recycled paper
Cover illustration and design by Ginger Sedlarova
Interior design by Typesmith

Talonbooks acknowledges the financial support of the Canada Council for the
Arts, the Government of Canada through the Canada Book Fund, and the Province
of British Columbia through the British Columbia Arts Council and the Book
Publishing Tax Credit.

Rights to *The Piano Teacher: A Healing Key*, in whole or in part, in any medium by
any group, amateur or professional, are retained by the author. Interested persons are
requested to contact the author care of Talonbooks at info@talonbooks.com.

LIBRARY AND ARCHIVES CANADA CATALOGUING IN PUBLICATION

Title: The piano teacher : a healing key / a play by Dorothy Dittrich ; foreword by
Yvette Nolan ; introduction by Rachel Ditor.
Names: Dittrich, Dorothy, 1960– author.
Description: A play | Nolan, Yvette, writer of foreword. | Ditor, Rachel, writer of
introduction.
Identifiers: Canadiana 20210322330 | ISBN 9781772014020 (softcover)
Classification: LCC PS8607.I88 P53 2022 | DDC C812/.6—dc23

For all those who have worked
through a difficult passage

It takes strength to make your way
through grief, to grab hold of life
and let it pull you forward.

—**Patti Davis**, *The Long Goodbye:*
  Memories of My Father (2005)

The reality is that you will grieve forever.
You will not "get over" the loss of a loved
one; you will learn to live with it. You
will heal and you will rebuild yourself
around the loss you have suffered.
You will be whole again, but you will
never be the same. Nor should you be
the same, nor would you want to.

—**Elisabeth Kübler-Ross** and **David Kessler**,
  On Grief and Grieving: Finding the Meaning of
  Grief through the Five Stages of Loss (1992)

Foreword

BY YVETTE NOLAN

The first time I read *The Piano Teacher*, I thought it was unutterably beautiful. Dorothy was grappling with so many ideas that resonated with me: art as medicine, moving on after great loss, the experience of grief. Like Elaine, the piano teacher of the title, I believe in the healing power of art, that art is what makes this life bearable.

Everybody experiences loss at some point, and it is impossible to compare one's pain to another's. Each of us finds our way to deal with the grief and to continue to choose life, the way Erin must in the play. The past two years of the COVID-19 pandemic – these *anni horribiles* – have made loss more immediate and more ubiquitous. After the initial shock of the globe locking down, the whole world began to enumerate the losses, and on the heels of that reckoning came the grieving. But do you remember the musicians on balconies, in those early days, locked down under quarantine, playing together, singing across courtyards and cities and continents? Singing to connect, to create community, to inspire hope.

Dorothy's play is a meditation on loss and grief, yes, but it is also an investigation into the role of the teacher. Elaine is generous and inventive, a careful listener. She is an incredible teacher because of how she connects with each of her students, not the least of whom is the fragile, fractured Erin. Elaine learns from her students, of course she does, because to teach is to learn twice, but she's no less a teacher for her humility in recognizing the lesson.

There is a moment in the play when Erin talks about a piece of music: Aaron Copland's *Appalachian Spring*. In the premiere production, when Erin thought of the piece, a sound cue fired and filled the theatre with Copland's classical composition, and we were there with her inside the music. The moment took my breath away. When I was rereading the script for this foreword, I came upon this same scene on the page, and I was transported to the moment again. Elaine asks Erin what Copland's music means to her, and Erin talks about the first time she heard the piece:

> I thought, this man has found a way to make us hear the landscape and the space around it. He's given it a voice.

This, to me, is the magic of what Dorothy has accomplished in *The Piano Teacher*. Somehow, she managed to translate into words on a page how music works, what it is, how it feels. Writing about how music transforms those who play it and those who listen to it, she offers us the chance to watch the characters in her play stumbling towards healing through art.

Introduction

BY RACHEL DITOR

Dorothy and I have a long-running joke about co-writing and performing the world's longest and most nonsensical play ever. (Don't worry, *The Piano Teacher* is not that play.) It starts with the two of us rappelling down the theatre walls, heavily armed, and then sitting down for an aimless chat that makes no reference to our dramatic entrance and features us getting distracted mid-conversation by trivial things, like where we bought our socks. We chat about minor health complaints, zone out, wonder what her cat Frankie is doing at home alone, and try to lead audience singalongs to songs for which we don't know the lyrics. Riffing on this would reliably crack us up.

And we needed to laugh.

The Piano Teacher is both a tough and beautiful landscape to inhabit. It's a gorgeous, moving story about vulnerability in relationships and the ability of music to move us through grief. When I think of the world of these characters, I always imagine the way frost creeps across a windowpane. Delicate, spiky trails of frozen water branching out, claiming more and more space until the view outside is hidden. Press a warm fingertip to the glass and melt a tiny view to the ice garden outside. To enter this play is to enter a frozen landscape on the verge of thawing. If you are still and patient, you will hear the slow dripping of the icicles starting to melt, feel the snowy ground shift slightly under your weight, and watch your hot breath turn to fog. If you are impatient, you might kick at the snow, curse to break the hushed quiet, and wish for the change of seasons to come NOW because nothing is happening! And in doing that, you'd miss ... everything.

Be patient with *The Piano Teacher*. Its jewels are revealed when you take a moment to stand still and pay attention to the world around and within ourselves. Take your time with this story and you will hear a seismic shift in the scrape of moving the piano bench closer to the keys, feel the almost unbearable weight of a simple greeting.

The Piano Teacher also delivers lush scores freshly illuminated by the most brilliant and user-friendly mini music-appreciation course. Elaine is a funny, warm, engaging guide. Her lessons hold true delights for both music lovers and those of us who tried and failed to find a passion for music under the gaze of an unforgiving teacher. And through Erin, our celebrated pianist, we travel from winter to spring with finely articulated emotional nuance, yielding a release that was palpable in the house every night as the audience remained in their seats long after the lights came up.

I always say to writers and students that a play is a conversation between a writer and an audience. The script is the playwright's offer – let's talk about *this*. Powerful writing is often generated from a need to investigate an idea, an image, a feeling. It often takes years to really finish writing a play, so that passion to understand, to wrestle with a subject, is a necessary engine, powering the writer back to the computer through endless rewrites. Dorothy's tenacity has provided us all with rich rewards. She generously invites us to pull up a chair, have a cup of tea, and engage in an exploratory conversation about grief and healing. Not to worry, you are in excellent hands – your host has a good sense of humour, compassion to spare, and stunning music for the journey.

The Piano Teacher

A Healing Key

Production History

The Piano Teacher was first produced by the Arts Club Theatre Company at the BMO Theatre Centre in Vancouver, British Columbia, from April 26 to May 14 with the following cast and crew:

ELAINE	Caitriona Murphy
ERIN	Megan Leitch
TOM	Kamyar Pazandeh
Director	Yvette Nolan
Producer	Bill Millerd
Stage Manager	Allison Spearin
Lighting Designer	Kyla Gardiner
Set Designer	David Roberts
Costume Designer	Jennifer Darbellay
Sound Designer	Patrick Pennefather
Dramaturge	Rachel Ditor

Characters

ELAINE: a warm, devoted, and classically trained piano teacher. Arthritis has forced her to give up her career as a performer.

ERIN: a successful pianist with a promising future. She has been unable to play the piano since the loss of both her husband and son.

TOM: a builder. Although he works outside the arts sector and never had the opportunity to attend lessons, he has a deep love of music. He is, in his own way, an artist.

Production Note

Both Erin and Elaine play the piano in the play; however, being able to play the piano is not a requirement. The roles were written for actors, so the musical pieces are very simple and played only briefly. Of these two roles, Elaine has the most playing to do. Some background playing the piano would be helpful but is not necessary. These pieces can be learned by the actors for the production.

Setting

Two homes combined into one. Elaine's living room, also used as her teaching space, opens to an area with a couch and a piano. This section of her home flows into the kitchen, which is represented by a breakfast bar. The breakfast bar contains a countertop with a sink. Below are cupboards that hold a teapot, cups, and various props, including the pie and toolbox. A table and chairs separate the breakfast bar and living room.

A set of stairs by the kitchen become part of Erin's home. The stairs lead to a platform landing, which has another set of stairs leading to a bedroom. This area is not lit to begin with.

Erin and Elaine share the piano and kitchen. Elaine's home is the living room with the piano, the couch, and the kitchen. Erin's home is the piano, the kitchen, and the stairs, as well as the landing and the upper level with a bedroom.

Act I

MUSIC CUE: Second movement (Andantino ed
innocentemente) of Haydn's Piano Trio no. 45 in E-flat
Major, Hob. XV:29, performed by the Beaux Arts Trio

*The music fades as the lights go up on **ELAINE**. She is
standing centre stage, giving a lecture.*

ELAINE

So. I am a piano teacher. You've come for a lesson. The first thing I
want to know is why. I mean, you want to learn to play, but there's
usually more to it than that.

You might say, "I took lessons when I was a kid," "I studied for
years and I can't play anything," or maybe this is a whole new
adventure for you. Regardless, whatever your reasons, there are
feelings involved, and those feelings are all going to come into
the lessons.

For me, music is a world, and in that world, there are rules and
systems and relationships. (*going to the piano*) In fact, music is
nothing but relationship – one note to the next, chords, scales,
keys – whole families of notes that belong together – or don't. The
dissonance of two notes that sit side by side (*playing a B and a C
together*) is brought into harmony by adding a third note. Add a
fourth and you have a peaceful community. (*playing a C major
seventh chord*) It's breathtaking.

And, like music, teaching is a relationship. Anyway, that's a bit
of my approach. You have to find yours – as future teachers.
And when you do, you have to be ready to let it go and change
everything because no two students are alike, no two days are alike
and oh, just when you're feeling on top of it, the student you have
absolutely no preparation for will arrive. And, I'm getting ahead
of myself.

*The lights go up on **ERIN** entering her home. She
takes off her coat and hangs it on a wall hook, then*

takes a man's sweater and puts it on as she heads into the kitchen.

ERIN

(*to Kevin, her late husband*) Well, that was quite an afternoon. Certainly not what I expected. I thought I was going to be trapped in an overcrowded basement for hours listening to children hammer their way through Beethoven, Schumann, Bach's *Notebook*, Mendelssohn's *Songs without Words*, the Impromptus. All those old chestnuts, but no. No one played any of them.

ERIN makes herself something to eat as ELAINE continues to speak.

ELAINE

Music is a language. I tell my students they need to learn to speak it, not just play it. Anyone can play music, but not everyone can communicate with it. When we play music, we're communicating the essence of who we are, and I believe if we communicate honestly from the heart, we can actually say something.

ERIN

I'm sure Sarah invited me just to get me out of the house. Sarah being kind. She has no idea how hard it is, but I have to say, I'm glad I went.

ELAINE

(*going to the piano and continuing to address the audience*) Music played from the heart speaks to the heart. It's healing. (*playing a note and then a scale*) Simple. Tiny little steps. Twelve notes. Infinite possibilities.

ERIN

It was really quite different. Very loose. There were only six or seven students and they ranged from five to about sixty years old. A boy played the piano for a young man who sang, and then a middle-aged woman played three songs she had written, which were quite good, and then her husband played blues. Maya

8

was amazing. She's gifted; she played Mozart. Just beautiful.
So delicate. You would have loved it. The best was the five-year-
old who didn't play at all. She said, "I learned a bunch of songs,"
and sat down. And everyone clapped. I thought that was brilliant.
Imagine the freedom, Kevin. Imagine being given the space not
to play. After the recital everyone stayed for dinner. I didn't. I just
couldn't.

ELAINE
Students don't always know what they've accomplished, and you
can't always put it in words that they'll hear or understand, so I
have a party, a ritual. No stress. They do something and we see
them do it.

ERIN
The whole thing was freeing, not just the recital, but the teacher
too. She was so... with her students... even the kid who didn't play.
She didn't push; she just let her find her way, and she did. The
minute the recital ended, that little girl went straight to the piano
and played while everyone was talking. It was beautiful.

ELAINE
So now this is the point I jumped ahead to. This little party, this
ritual I have every year, is where I met the student I was not
prepared for. I knew who she was. It isn't every day that a... well,
a famous pianist comes to your home to watch a little recital.
No one else recognized her, and she clearly didn't want attention
in that way.

ERIN
I felt almost normal. Safe.

ERIN picks up her phone.

ELAINE
Imagine my surprise when she called a month later.

ELAINE answers her phone.

ERIN
Hello, Elaine? This is Erin Bruchmann. I came to your recital to
see Maya play.

ELAINE
Yes, I remember.

ERIN
I'm calling to see if I can come by and speak to you.

ELAINE
Oh. Of course. When would you like to come over?

ERIN
My schedule is flexible right now. Tell me when works for you.

ELAINE
How's tomorrow morning?

ERIN
Tomorrow morning is fine.

ELAINE
Good. See you then.

> *Both hang up. ELAINE puts her phone down slowly,
> thoughtfully, and stares at it.*

ERIN
Good. This is good.

> *ERIN puts on her coat and walks down the stairs as
> ELAINE speaks.*

ELAINE
Well, I didn't know what to think. I couldn't imagine what she
wanted, but you know, I didn't want to press her over the phone.
The phone is tricky. I assumed it was about Maya.

> *There's a knock at the door. It's ERIN, holding a
> raincoat over her arm.*

ELAINE
Hello.

ERIN
Hi.

ELAINE
Please. Come in.

> *ERIN enters but pauses inside the door, hesitant.*
> *ELAINE motions for her to enter fully. ERIN slowly*
> *walks in and stands awkwardly between the piano and*
> *the couch.*

ERIN
Okay. Thank you.

> *ERIN considers the piano bench, then sits on the couch*
> *instead. ELAINE watches ERIN and begins a slow,*
> *friendly conversation, simple and easy, aware that*
> *ERIN seems fragile. ELAINE's manner is light and*
> *kind, intended to draw ERIN out, to make her feel*
> *comfortable and relaxed.*

ELAINE
Can I hang up your coat?

ERIN
No, thank you.

ELAINE
It does look like it might rain, though they didn't predict
it, did they?

ERIN
I don't know. I didn't hear anything.

ELAINE
Well, it so often doesn't matter what they predict, does it? I mean,
the weather does whatever it wants.

ERIN
Yes, it does.

ELAINE
I don't listen anymore. I just go by my hands.

ERIN
Your hands?

ELAINE
They hurt when it's going to rain. The singular silver lining to arthritis. (*going to the kitchen while still talking*) I'm making tea, would you like a cup?

ERIN
No thank you. I'm fine for now.

ELAINE
Okay.

> *ELAINE pours water into the teapot and brings it to the table on a tray as she is speaking.*

ELAINE
So, you're friends with Maya.

ERIN
Yes. I've known her mother for years. We went to university together.

ELAINE
She is a very talented musician herself, isn't she? Maya's mother.

ERIN
Yes, she is.

ELAINE
Of course, it makes sense that Maya is so gifted.

ERIN
Yes. (*pause*) I enjoyed the recital very much.

ELAINE
It was quite an honour to have you here, Miss Bruchmann.

ERIN
Erin. Please, call me Erin.

ELAINE
Erin. Right. I was… I am so very sorry for your loss.

ERIN
Thank you.

ELAINE
Well. (*pause*) Is Maya unhappy with her lessons?

ERIN
No. I don't think so. She plays all the time. Why do you ask?

ELAINE
I ask because I assume you've come to discuss Maya and honestly, when a meeting is asked for, it's usually about a problem.

ERIN
Oh no. No, I didn't come about Maya. They don't even know I'm here. No, I've come for myself.

ELAINE
Yourself.

ERIN
Yes. I've come to ask if you would work with me.

ELAINE
Oh.

ERIN
If you have space in your schedule.

ELAINE
Oh.

ERIN

Do you have time?

ELAINE

Yes. Yes, of course I have time. I don't really know what you mean by "work with" you. What are you looking for?

ERIN

I can't seem to... play anymore. I mean, I can play, but I haven't since... I can't. I can't play. I can't even sit at the piano.

ELAINE

I see.

ERIN

I thought it would pass. I thought I'd just start playing again, but I just... it's...

ELAINE

You know, it makes sense. It's not an unimaginable reaction to your loss.

ERIN

I know.

ELAINE

I am certainly not making a comparison, but I want to tell you, when my marriage ended, I didn't listen to music for months. I didn't play, either. I know divorce is a choice, but my heart was still broken, and music goes right to the heart. It's just... I'm sure you'll come through this if you let your grief run its course.

ERIN

I don't have time for that. I need to play and I cannot sit at the piano. I can't touch it. It's been almost two years. I'm going to lose my hands if I don't do something now.

ELAINE

Forgive me, but have you seen a grief counsellor? Or a therapist?

ERIN
    Yes. Both.

ELAINE
    Don't you think –

ERIN
    I felt safe here.

ELAINE
    That's a wonderful compliment, but Miss Bruchmann –

ERIN
    Erin.

ELAINE
    Erin. I teach music. I'm not a therapist.

ERIN
    I know. I don't want a therapist. I want to play the piano. I need you to teach me. Help me play the piano again.

ELAINE
    You know how to play.

ERIN
    But I can't. What's the difference?

MUSIC CUE: First movement (Andante) of Haydn's Piano Trio no. 39 in G Major, Hob. XV:25, performed by the Gryphon Trio

---

ELAINE steps into the living room as ERIN gets up and leaves. She climbs the stairs to her home and stops on the landing to look at the wall for a moment before climbing the second set of stairs. The lights fade on ERIN.

ELAINE

Of course I agreed to work with her. Of course. Even though I had no idea what to do. She said she felt safe in my home. What else is there?

The music fades as the lights go up on ERIN entering ELAINE's home.

ELAINE

Have you brought something to work on?

ERIN

Yes. I brought a couple of things.

ELAINE

May I see?

ERIN

(*holding up a flat valise to indicate the music inside*) I brought a book of Haydn sonatas.

ERIN stands stiffly for a moment before moving instinctively to the piano. She looks at ELAINE and then stands by the piano bench with her back to the keyboard.

ELAINE

Lovely. Great. How would you like to start with a cup of tea?

ERIN

Yes, thank you. That would be nice.

ELAINE

We have plenty of time. (*making tea, aware that ERIN is uncomfortable*) Would you like to sit there (*pointing to the couch*) or at the table?

ERIN

Here is good.

ERIN sits on the couch.

ELAINE
I've always loved Haydn. He was so innovative, especially with transitions. So. What were you working on last?

ERIN
We just finished. It was Haydn. The quintet had played the winter concert.

ELAINE
What else?

ERIN
Pardon?

ELAINE
Haydn was in your repertoire. What were you working on?

ERIN
Oh, right. I was working on Bartók's *Folk Dances.*

ELAINE
Great.

ERIN
I was planning to do a whole series of Bartók.

ELAINE
With the quintet?

ERIN
No, solo. I was also working on the Copeland Concerto. I had been asked to play with the symphony.

ELAINE
My God, what an opportunity.

ERIN
It was. I cancelled, of course.

ELAINE
Of course.

ERIN
(*pause*) We had been talking about doing a recording and then a tour. It was pretty big. We hadn't decided on the details yet, but we were planning.

ELAINE
Is the symphony still waiting for you?

ERIN
They left the door open. But that was two years ago.

ELAINE
What about the recording?

ERIN
It's still there, waiting.

ELAINE
I saw you play once, you know. You played Schubert with the quintet and then one of the trio sonatas.

ERIN
The E-flat. That would have been with my husband.

ELAINE
It was… wonderful.

ERIN
Thank you.

ELAINE
(*pause*) Well. I've been thinking about how we're going to be doing this "lesson," as you call it, since we spoke last.

ERIN
Me too.

ELAINE
I mean, I don't know quite where to start, Erin. It's a bit...

ERIN
I'm just another piano student.

ELAINE
Right. So that being the case, I think it's best to do what I always do with a new student – talk a bit.

ELAINE gestures for ERIN to join her at the table to talk and drink tea.

ERIN
Great.

ELAINE
Okay. Is there any music you don't like?

ERIN
No, I don't think so.

ELAINE
Good. That's great, lots of room to play. How about composers? Are there any you don't care for?

ERIN
Beethoven.

ELAINE
Oh. Really?

ERIN
Can't stand him.

ELAINE
Oh.

ERIN
Is that a problem?

ELAINE

Absolutely not. Why don't you like him if you don't mind me asking? Just curious.

ERIN

Too big, too loud, too much. Plus, I've always thought he was probably a bit of a bastard.

ELAINE

Oh. Well that's a new one for me. So. No Beethoven.

ERIN

I'm sorry...

ELAINE

No, no. Don't be. I'm not averse to a strong critique. I've heard a lot of reasons not to play Beethoven, but I've never heard that. I like it. The possibilities. I see the documentary on PBS: "Beethoven: A Bit of a Bastard – The Early Years."

ERIN

You must think I'm an idiot.

ELAINE

On the contrary, I feel soothed.

ERIN

Why?

ELAINE

Because I would never play Chopin.

ERIN

Really?

ELAINE

Really. His music reminds me of clammy hands. Cold clammy hands. I've never told anyone that before, you know, because you can't hate Chopin. It's like hating baby chicks or something, but I do, so here we are. Free.

ERIN
Free?

ELAINE
Completely. The truth sets us free, right? Being honest is a part of playing music.

ERIN
My husband always said I had a flair for the lyrical, mercurial passages but that my hand was a delicate hand, not built for Beethoven, which I think has some truth to it. I mean... anyway, I don't like him, so there you go.

ELAINE
I think Bartók can be every bit as demanding. When is the last time you played?

ERIN
That afternoon.

ELAINE
And you haven't sat at the piano since?

ERIN
No.

> *ELAINE stands, thinking for a moment. She puts her tea down on the table, moves a chair aside, and strides to the piano. ERIN watches.*

ELAINE
Okay. Let's start with the bench.

ERIN
Pardon?

> *ELAINE picks up the bench and places it at the kitchen table.*

ELAINE
We'll start with the bench. (*patting the bench*) Come have a seat.
We'll finish our tea here.

ERIN
Okay.

> *ERIN gets up and walks carefully to the bench. She
> is hesitant; it's hard for her to sit. She has to work for
> it. This all happens while they talk. It takes some time
> until she pulls the bench back from the table so that she
> can sit. It's the same way she would move the bench if
> she were sitting at the piano. This is physical memory,
> automatic. She hesitates again. She moves to the front
> of the bench and sits, pushing the bench slightly back
> with her legs to make more room. Again, an unconscious
> habit, the same as sitting at a piano. She sits and wipes
> her hands on her pants before placing them on the table.
> While this is happening, ELAINE pours tea and refills
> ERIN's cup, talking the whole time.*

ELAINE
So. Bartók and Copland. A completely different track from the
quintet repertoire.

ERIN
Yes, exactly. They're truer to my musical tastes.

ELAINE
Really.

ERIN
I was very interested in all things modern when I first started
my career, when Kevin and I met, in fact. I was fascinated by the
American sound. There was this very exciting thing going on,
as though sound was up for grabs. There were no rules.

ELAINE
And tons of rules.

ERIN

Exactly. (*pause*) Kevin was an extraordinary musician. He had such incredible discipline. (*smiling*) And soul.

ELAINE

Did he share your interest in twentieth-century music?

ERIN

Oh, of course he did. You know, you play it all, you appreciate it all.

ELAINE

But you don't "love" it all.

ERIN

No. Not fully. I mean, how can you? (*pause*) Kevin loved the classical world. The order, the structure, the form.

ELAINE

But not you?

ERIN

Yes, oh yes. I love that world, I do, but I also love the messiness and the earthiness of Bartók.

ELAINE

So you didn't play Bartók with the quintet? I mean, there's plenty of material.

ERIN

Oh sure, Bartók was in the repertoire, and Kevin and I played the Andante, for piano and violin, which is so beautiful...

ELAINE

And definitely not the Sonata for Violin and Piano.

ERIN

Exactly. (*smiling again*) No, Kevin wouldn't have anything to do with the Sonata.

ELAINE
I have to say, I don't have much interest in twentieth-century music. My great love is Bach. Not to play, to listen to. Otherwise, I'm mainly a fan of old standards and blues.

ERIN
Really?

ELAINE
You're surprised.

ERIN
Yes, I am.

ELAINE
Fair enough. I guess my tastes aren't why you're here. Let me ask you a question. What is Copland for you? One word.

ERIN
Space.

MUSIC CUE: First section (Very slowly; in A Major) of Aaron Copland's *Appalachian Spring*, performed by the New York Philharmonic Orchestra

---

ELAINE
Yes.

ERIN
Which doesn't mean it isn't intense.

ELAINE
Oh, I think space is very intense. Especially if you think about what's in the space.

ERIN
Exactly.

ELAINE

So Bartók: messy and earthy. And Copland: space.

ERIN

Right. The first time I heard Copland I was about fifteen. It was the *Appalachian Spring* suite, of course. I thought, this man has found a way to make us hear the landscape and the space around it. He's given it a voice. (*pause*) I've always craved space. Too much up here. (*indicating her head*)

> *The music fades out. They sit in silence for a long moment, then* ERIN *stands and puts her coat on to leave.*

ERIN

So what should I work on this week?

ELAINE

Nothing. Don't work on anything. The only thing I want you to do this week is touch the piano, yours at home. You don't have to play anything. You don't even have to touch the keys. Just touch the piano every day.

ERIN

Okay.

ELAINE

I'll see you next week.

> *While* ELAINE *says what follows,* ERIN *enters her home and sets the valise down on the table by the entrance. She takes off her coat, hangs it up, then removes a man's sweater from the hook and puts it on. She goes into the kitchen and takes out a plate, which she fills with cookies.*

ELAINE

(*to the audience*) We maintain our relationships with the dead. We talk to the dead, wear their clothes, take up their hobbies.

ERIN

(*to Kevin, offstage*) I'm managing. I have to, but I still can't think straight.

ERIN takes out a mug and pours herself some tea.

ERIN

Honestly... have to stay right here... this moment.

ELAINE

It's common for a person to take up an interest or hobby that they once complained about or disliked.

ERIN

Just the task at hand...

ELAINE

The widow who never shared her husband's interest in golf suddenly becomes an avid golfer when her husband dies.

ERIN

I had my lesson today. Bit different. I don't know. We'll see.

ERIN bites into a cookie and leans against the counter to think.

ELAINE

Sometimes a person will reject everything about their previous life, almost like it didn't happen.

ERIN

I think you'd like her.

ELAINE

Most people stay attached until they get strong enough to let go.

ERIN
How am I going to play music?

> *ERIN carries the plate and tea upstairs. ELAINE moves into the kitchen where ERIN has just been and begins to clean the dishes. She puts the kettle back on the counter. The kitchen is now hers.*

ELAINE
(*to the audience*) It has taken me years to work through the loss of my hands. I had to accept the fact that the potential I was born with simply wasn't going to be realized. Physical pain, emotional pain, we have to live with it, that's a fact. How we do it is the art, I suppose. She said, "I know how to play but I can't. What's the difference?" (*pause*) Who knows, perhaps she came to the right place.

MUSIC CUE: First movement (Allegro) of Haydn's Piano Sonata no. 59 in E-flat Major, Hob. XVI:49, performed by Vladimir Horowitz

---

> *ERIN enters Elaine's house. She calls Elaine's name over the piano music.*

ERIN
Hello? Elaine?

> *No one answers. ERIN stands still and listens for a moment, then looks at the piano keyboard. She stretches out her hand and touches the keys. ELAINE enters.*

ELAINE
Oh, you're here. Lovely. (*turning off the music with a remote*) Sorry, I was doing my taxes. I always play this when I'm doing my taxes.

ERIN

(*laughing*) I would not have put Horowitz and Haydn together with taxes.

ELAINE

Humour. They both had a delightful sense of humour.

ERIN

It's November.

ELAINE

Yes.

ERIN

So you're either very late or very early.

ELAINE

I'm very early. I always do my taxes in November so that I don't have to feel overwhelmed and disgusted in the spring. How are you? How was your week?

ERIN

Quiet but fine.

ELAINE

Quiet but fine is good.

> *ELAINE sets the teapot on the table with a couple of mugs.*

ELAINE

Did you practise at all?

ERIN

Nope.

ELAINE

That's good.

ERIN

I touched the piano, though, as instructed.

ELAINE
Fantastic. What a disciplined student you are. How was it?

ERIN
Not bad. It needed dusting.

ELAINE
Good. Okay, so today the bench stays at the piano, but you keep your back to the keyboard.

ERIN
Really?

ELAINE
We're just trying things. Let's not think too much or it'll get weird.

ERIN
Okay.

> *ELAINE hands ERIN a cup of tea and then returns to the breakfast bar.*

ELAINE
Highlight of your week?

ERIN
My history class. I teach a music history class at the university.

ELAINE
You enjoy teaching?

ERIN
Very much, which is new. I haven't really connected to teaching until now.

ELAINE
Life changes us.

> *ERIN remains near the piano bench sipping her tea while ELAINE sets a couple of plates on the counter.*

ELAINE

So, in the interest of life and art and change, I have a
surprise for you.

ERIN

You do? What is it?

ELAINE takes a pie from the cupboard.

ELAINE

I've made pie.

ERIN

I love pie. What kind is it?

ELAINE

Cherry.

ERIN

That's my favourite.

ELAINE

I know.

ELAINE takes a pie cutter from the drawer.

ERIN

How do you know my favourite pie?

*ELAINE starts to cut the pie. The crust is hard, so the
pie falls apart a bit. She has trouble getting it on the
plate. She continues to talk while she works.*

ELAINE

Maya told me at one of her lessons. You were going to her house
for dinner and she and her mother were making pie for dessert.
She was very excited. She said, "My aunty Erin is coming for
dinner. We're making cherry pie. It's her favourite." Look who
Aunty Erin turns out to be.

ERIN
I remember that dinner. Kevin was on the road. Terrence was with me. That was almost three years ago. You've got quite a memory.

ELAINE
Yes. Both a blessing and a curse.

ERIN
It's useful for a musician to have a good memory.

ELAINE
(*feeling both pleased and shy at the comment*) I don't really think of myself as a musician anymore. I think of myself as a teacher.

ERIN
You're still a musician.

ELAINE
Thank you. (*handing the pie to ERIN*) And here you are.

ERIN takes the plate and sits down with it on the piano bench, her back to the keyboard.

ERIN
Thanks.

ELAINE
Sorry, it kind of broke.

ERIN
It's the taste that matters.

ELAINE
I've never made pie before.

ERIN
You're kidding.

ERIN cuts into the pie and struggles a bit with the crust. ELAINE gets herself a slice, oblivious to ERIN's struggle.

ELAINE
No, I'm not much of a baker. My mother, now she could bake.

ERIN
(*smiling and taking a bite*) It's delicious.

ELAINE
Good. Who would have imagined we'd be sitting having cherry pie together?

ERIN
In November. What a treat.

ELAINE
Exactly. (*trying to cut into her slice, less subtle about the crust struggle*) Good God, this crust is like floor tile.

ERIN
(*laughing*) It's not that bad. The filling is delicious.

ELAINE
Just eat the filling, then. (*pause*) You'll think I'm crazy, but I wanted you to have something sweet at the piano.

ERIN
I don't think you're crazy. I think it's lovely. (*taking another bite*) You know, (*pause*) Maya and Terrence were good friends.

ELAINE
Oh, but of course they would be. I didn't even think...

ERIN
I know. (*setting her plate on her lap*) It's too much.

ELAINE
Maya is an important little person.

ERIN
She's pretty precious. (*pause*) Her mother and I played in the quintet.

ELAINE
I know.

ERIN
Right. Of course. (*pause*) They want to know if I'm coming back. They said they're willing to wait a bit longer, but they want a decision. I understand. I mean, they've already been so patient. They have to move on.

> *ELAINE goes to the piano and takes ERIN's plate.*

ELAINE
Do you want to go back?

ERIN
I don't know. I know I want to play again.

ELAINE
Then you will.

ERIN
I'm glad you're so certain.

> *The lights shift. ERIN stands and moves to the side of the piano. ELAINE remains at the table.*

ELAINE
(*to the audience*) I had no clue what to do. No idea at all. All I could think of was comfort. I may not have had much to teach her, but I could listen.

MUSIC CUE: Third movement (Topogó / Pe loc) of Bartók's *Romanian Folk Dances*, Sz. 56, BB 68, for piano

---

The lights shift again. It is another day, another lesson. The music slowly fades.

ERIN

(*enthusiastic, lighter*) I had a schedule at one time that was so full, so crazy, I honestly don't know how I did it. But I loved it. It was my life. You know, I could remember hours of music, pages and pages of it. I must've had endless stamina. Now I can barely make it to the grocery store. I'm exhausted by 8 p.m. And I can't remember what I'm doing half the time.

ELAINE

Grief is humbling. It's all consuming. It takes everything.

ERIN

Have you experienced trauma? I mean, traumatic loss?

ELAINE

I have certainly experienced loss. But nothing in the way you have.

ERIN

(*calmly and quietly, almost detached*) There's a point where you unhook from the world. You just... unhook. Your world is gone. It's just... I can't even tell you what it's like.

ELAINE

I would think that's half the problem.

ERIN

Yes. Yes, it is. And when I try to explain it, I hear myself coming up with these idiotic analogies, like getting off the bus at the wrong stop. Getting off at the wrong stop. Jesus. I actually said that to someone. I said, "I feel disoriented, like I got off the bus at the wrong stop. I don't know where I am and I feel lost." Which is true, except it's more like getting off the bus at the wrong stop after having your head blown to bits and handed to you in a paper bag. But you can't say that, so you try to explain in gentle terms so people don't think you're being too dramatic.

ELAINE

Be dramatic. Explain it to me.

ERIN

Okay. Every day I wake up feeling like I've been broken.
Sometimes when I first wake up, I don't know where I am. Images
start to flood my mind. It's like being stuck in an endless loop of
looking back, and it's always perfect, the past is perfect and we
were always happy. I hear voices. I hear my husband's laugh, I see
my son out the kitchen window. I know it's nostalgia, but that
doesn't help. Sometimes I have actual pain in my heart. It feels like
it's been pierced. Then I get up and make coffee. Sometimes I feel
nothing at all. It's better when I feel nothing. At night, when I go
to bed, all that pain comes back. That's it. That's my life. There's
nothing fluid or easy in it. It just saws along choppy and scraping
and jagged. Things don't make sense to me anymore. Do you
understand what I'm saying?

ELAINE

I think so.

ERIN

Kevin was my home. Now he's gone. Now I'm homeless.

The lights shift as ERIN *gets up and leaves.* ELAINE
*goes to the piano and begins to play a simple piece.
She stops, flexes her fingers, then speaks. Through this
monologue, we see* ERIN *arrive at her home, set her
keys in a dish by the door, take off her coat, and slip on
her husband's sweater. She checks her phone and plugs
in the kettle. After she makes tea, she slowly climbs the
stairs to the landing. The lights fade on* ERIN.

ELAINE

(*to the audience*) Music is patterns. Like this.

*She plays a five-note pattern, then raises it a semitone
and looks at the audience.*

ELAINE

You see? Or this.

35

She plays a left-hand pattern.

ELAINE

This pattern is a broken chord. That's all. It's called an Alberti bass. It's a way of sustaining on chord under a melody.

She plays the first four bars of Mozart's Piano Sonata no. 16 in C Major, K. 545.

ELAINE

Sweet, charming. (*pause*) And of course, this.

She plays the first few bars of the first movement (Adagio sostenuto) of Beethoven's Piano Sonata no. 14 in C-sharp Minor, op. 27, no. 2 (the Moonlight Sonata*).*

ELAINE

The broken chord sustains with such power. The chord's unbroken sounds... banal, bare ... but this? This is sublime.

To illustrate her point, ELAINE plays the broken chord as a solid chord. She plays the repeated melody over the solid chord just briefly.

ELAINE

Isn't it remarkable how something that's broken can be so strong, compelling, beautiful, and so much more interesting? The broken chord is like a container for the melody – it holds it.

When she starts with the broken chord again, she starts where the melody begins, using her right hand. This whole "teaching" segment spans the first twelve to sixteen bars before the music cue takes over.

MUSIC CUE: First movement (Adagio sostenuto) of Ludwig van Beethoven's Piano Sonata no. 14 in C-sharp Minor, op. 27, no. 2 (*Moonlight Sonata*)

ELAINE

(*to the audience*) It allows the melody to work itself through. It supports without imposing itself.

> *ELAINE picks up the piano bench and moves it to the kitchen table.*

ELAINE

We behave in patterns, consciously or unconsciously. Sometimes, when I think about our lessons, I think of us weaving a tapestry of sorts, creating a new fabric and new patterns for us both. Patterns, rituals, and stories. They hold us, give us shape and form. They give us a way to move through life. They can hold us while we heal, contain us, until we're strong enough to move forward.

> *The music fades and the lights shift. It's a new day. ERIN, relaxed, sits on the piano bench at the kitchen table.*

ERIN

Have you always been a teacher?

ELAINE

No. I've done a number of things.

ERIN

Did you ever perform?

ELAINE

That's a long story, one I don't think we have time to get into. I have a student coming in a bit.

ERIN

Can you tell me a little? Twenty-five words or less?

ELAINE

I wanted to and did perform briefly, but then I learned I had a debilitating form of arthritis.

ERIN

Oh my God, Elaine. I'm sorry.

ELAINE

Yes, not good. I stopped playing for a long time. I travelled, fell in love, and got married.

ERIN

I'm sorry. I didn't think…

ELAINE

It's fine, Erin. I wouldn't have told you if it was still a problem. Now, I'm sorry, but my student will be here soon.

ERIN

Okay. (*standing*) You have a lot of students.

ELAINE

Yes.

ERIN

I teach one course and it's all I can handle. I'm afraid I'm not very productive these days.

ELAINE

Oh my God. Here's your daily affirmation. Look in the mirror, look into your eyes, and say: "I am a good person, and I am going to give myself a huge fucking break because I am in shock. I am in grief. I am shattered. Today, if I can manage a shower and have a couple of laughs, it will be a brilliant day." Repeat that four thousand times.

ERIN

(*going to the coat rack, laughing*) Thank you, doctor.

ELAINE

You're very welcome. What are you up to now?

ERIN

I'm not sure. Probably walk around a bit.

ELAINE

(*helping her with her coat*) Walk around a mall. It's bloody cold out.

ERIN

Don't worry. I'm not going to stay outdoors until hypothermia sets in.

ELAINE

Oh God, do I sound like that?

ERIN

It's nice. I like it.

ELAINE

Good, because I have a thought about this walking around that you do.

ERIN

Yes?

ELAINE

Actually it's about your place. It's just an idea, but you don't like going home, or even being there, and you need to be there to practise.

ERIN

I thought I'm not supposed to practise.

ELAINE

Eventually, you'll have to, so maybe you just need to make a little change, like a painting or something, new furniture. There've been times in my life where even a new bath mat made a real difference.

ERIN

Frankly, I think I'd rather move than paint.

ELAINE
(*laughing*) I know what you mean.

> *ELAINE hands ERIN her gloves. ERIN puts them on.*

ERIN
You know, (*pause*) I could change the landing.

ELAINE
What?

ERIN
Our landing at home. (*hugging ELAINE, her spirit lifting*) Thank you. I'll see you next week.

ELAINE
I'll be here.

> *ELAINE gently closes the door after ERIN. ELAINE goes to the piano, pulls out a book of music, and opens it. She looks at the music and sets it on the piano bench. The lights fade on ELAINE's home and shift to ERIN's. She stands beside TOM at the foot of the stairs. They're both looking up at the wall at the top of the landing.*

TOM
So you want a window put in here.

ERIN
Yes.

TOM
(*climbing the stairs*) Well, that should be easy enough. (*tapping and studying the wall*) I don't see a problem.

ERIN
Good.

TOM
I'll need to see about wiring.

ERIN

Do you think it might not be possible?

TOM

Don't worry, we'll figure it out. Tell me what you're thinking.

ERIN

Well, I'm not sure exactly. I wanted to talk to you first. You can see it's a big landing, it's almost a room, but right now it's just dead space.

> *ERIN also climbs the stairs to the landing.*

TOM

Right.

ERIN

I've always seen myself in a chair by the window, a little table here, maybe a bookshelf. I thought this whole area could be like a reading room, or maybe just a place to sit.

TOM

I get it.

> *TOM steps back to survey the area.*

ERIN

You do?

TOM

I do. I have a couple of thoughts if you want them.

ERIN

Absolutely.

TOM

All right. The first one is (*kneeling*) start the window here (*indicating about a metre up the wall*) and then extend the sill out and make it into a seat.

ERIN

Cushions along the top.

TOM

Exactly. Then you can create a storage space under it or even a bookshelf. You know what I mean?

ERIN

Yes.

TOM

Or the other idea is that we go a bit bolder and have the window start here (*indicating about a foot from the floor*) and take it right up the wall.

ERIN

Oh.

TOM

Yeah. Just blow the whole wall out.

ERIN

Wow.

TOM

Is there anything to look at out there?

ERIN

A tree, the hedge.

TOM

Well, it's something to think about, anyway.

ERIN

Yes. It could be very nice.

TOM

When are you planning on getting this project underway?

ERIN

I'm hoping right away. Tomorrow, if you're free.

TOM

Tomorrow. (*laughing*) I don't know. You know it's January. Maybe not the best time to be cutting holes in the side of your house. Wait until the weather improves a bit.

ERIN

No. No, I'm not waiting. People wait for things and then... no.

TOM

Okay. I have a couple of jobs I'm finishing, but I'll see what I can figure out.

ERIN

Thank you.

TOM

It makes sense, you know. Why wait? Plus, winter's when you need light the most, right?

ERIN

Right.

> *TOM goes into his bag and retrieves a marker.*

TOM

I'll mark an outline so you can get an idea.

ERIN

That sounds great.

> *ERIN sits on the stairs and waits. TOM returns with a stepladder. He begins to work, marking lines on the wall while he talks.*

TOM

I was thinking, when you called, that I'd get a buddy of mine to help with this, but I think I can do it on my own. That will keep the costs down.

ERIN

A buddy.

TOM

Yes. What?

ERIN

Nothing. I like that word. It's sweet.

TOM

Oh.

ERIN

There was a song written in the twenties called "My Buddy." It's lovely.

TOM

Right. I know it.

ERIN

Oh?

TOM

Yeah, I like old music. Tin Pan Alley. I like bluegrass too. Do you play that piano downstairs?

ERIN

I used to. I don't these days, though.

TOM

I always wanted to play the piano.

ERIN

Maybe you'll learn one day.

TOM

Maybe I will. Why not, right? Never too late. Okay.

TOM starts to work on the window outline.

ERIN

When we first bought the house, my husband and I talked about doing some renovations. He said a window here wasn't a priority, which was his way of saying he didn't really like the idea. I fought for it, of course, but you know how it is. He didn't say no, it just didn't happen. I was really angry at him about that. It's crazy the things we get mad about... (*drifting*) and none of it matters, does it?

TOM

No, not really. (*pause*) But I like to have some background while I build something. A story. It makes it more fun. (*stopping his drawing*) You're divorced then?

ERIN

No.

TOM

Oh, I thought...

ERIN

I'm... My husband died.

TOM

Oh. Oh, I'm sorry. I didn't mean to...

ERIN

Please, it's okay. I brought it up.

TOM

Okay, (*returning to his drawing*) so that's the window with the seat.

ERIN

Right. Okay.

TOM

The other option is to start here (*drawing below the ledge*) and go to here.

TOM draws along the bottom and then up to the top of the window, basically a rectangle within a square.

He speaks while he works.

TOM

If you played Scrabble, you could play it here.

ERIN

You could.

TOM

Do you play Scrabble?

ERIN

No.

TOM

No? That's unheard of.

ERIN

Is it?

TOM

It certainly is. At least in my world it is.

ERIN

I'm not good at those kinds of games, word games, spelling. I don't think I'd be very good at it.

TOM

I, on the other hand, am. I am a very good Scrabble player.

ERIN

Are you?

TOM
It's more about knowing the tricks than skill or talent. You don't even have to be able to spell very well.

ERIN
(*speaking over his line*) Just like life.

TOM
Pardon?

ERIN
I said just like life. Knowing the tricks. It was meant to be a joke.

TOM
Oh. Right.

ERIN
But it wasn't funny, and I don't know why I said it. It's not something I'd normally say. Anyway, what did you say? I missed it.

TOM
I said you don't have to be able to spell very well.

ERIN
Right.

> *TOM finishes the window outline and steps back to look at it.*

TOM
Okay, so there's both windows.

> *ERIN studies the outlines.*

ERIN
I see.

TOM
(*stepping back to stand beside her*) Well, live with it a day or two and then give me a call when you've decided.

ERIN
I already know.

TOM
You want the big window, don't you?

ERIN
Yes.

TOM
Okay. I'll call around and see if I can get something close to keep the cost down.

ERIN
I don't care about costs.

TOM
You say that now.

ERIN
When can you start?

TOM
Let me sort out my schedule a bit, find out if there's a window in stock. If everything lines up, I'll try to start tomorrow.

ERIN
Thank you, that's wonderful.

TOM
(*picking up his bag to leave*) I'll check out both sizes just in case and get back to you.

ERIN
You're careful.

TOM
When I'm cutting a hole in a wall in the middle of winter, I tend towards caution. You never know, you might change your mind.

ERIN
No.

TOM

Decisive. Good. I like decisive.

> *TOM and ERIN both start down the stairs.*

TOM

I'll call you about tomorrow.

> *TOM exits. The lights shift to ELAINE's home. ERIN enters and heads to the piano bench, where she sits with her back to the keys.*

ELAINE

Knocking a hole in the wall in January. Good for you.

ERIN

To hell with the elements.

ELAINE

I have to say, I thought you meant having some carpet put in or moulding or something like that… and in the spring.

ERIN

So did Tom.

ELAINE

Tom?

ERIN

The guy who's doing the work.

ELAINE

Oh.

ERIN

Do you know what he said? He said, "I guess winter would be when you need light the most." Isn't that great?

ELAINE

It is. It's great and it's true and he's obviously smart enough to know that the customer is always right.

ERIN

I know. I'm sure it's just pure charm, but it was still nice to hear. (*pause*) You know what else? It's nice having someone in the house. Even if it's a workman I don't even know.

ELAINE

Is he there now?

ERIN

Yes.

ELAINE

Maybe you should go home.

ERIN

(*laughing*) No... Anyway, he's busy working.

ELAINE

Then you should definitely go home.

ERIN

I'm not ready for...

ELAINE

I know, I know. It's just fun to tease you.

ERIN

Clearly. (*still with her back to the piano, facing the room with her hands on her knees and back straight*) What are we working on today? I think we have the bench pretty much in hand, don't you?

ELAINE

So then why don't you turn around?

ERIN

Oh. Okay. (*looking at her hands and not moving*)

> *ELAINE continues to talk as she notices ERIN growing contracted, withdrawn. ERIN's energy seems smaller.*

ELAINE
It seems there's a lot of good strong energy around you.
New energy.

ERIN
(*still not moving*) Yes.

ELAINE
You don't have to...

ERIN
No, it's good... it's good.

ELAINE
We'll start with the bench out a bit. Okay?

ERIN
(*nodding*) Mm hmm.

ELAINE
(*gently*) Would you like me to sit with you?

ERIN
Yes.

> *ELAINE sits on the bench with ERIN. ELAINE faces
> the keyboard and sits straight, her hands in her lap.
> ERIN turns to face the keyboard as well. She also places
> her hands in her lap.*

ELAINE
That's all we're going to do today.

> *ERIN nods.*

ELAINE
Shall I play something?

ERIN
Okay.

ELAINE starts to play a turn-of-the-century waltz,
a folk song that's quiet and gentle – perhaps it's "Till We
Meet Again," a 1918 American popular song composed
by Richard A. Whiting, with lyrics by Raymond B. Egan.
The lights fade on the two women and shift to TOM on
a ladder in the landing. He is stapling a piece of clear
plastic over the area where the window is being put in.
ERIN enters her home and calls from the doorway.

ERIN

(*seeing the window and heading up the stairs*) Oh, wow.

TOM

Is it too much?

ERIN

No. It's great. It's so different. Even seeing it drawn doesn't give a sense of scale, does it?

TOM

(*looking at the window*) No, not really. That's why I didn't want to go through until you'd seen it and I had your approval.

ERIN

Approval granted.

TOM

Excellent. I'll go pick up the window now, then. I can have it in by tonight.

TOM leaves, and ERIN heads downstairs to the piano.
She touches the edge along the piano keys. She pulls
the bench out a bit and opens it. She extracts a piece of
music, looks at it, sets it on the piano's music stand, then
takes a couple of books out, opens one, and puts it on the
piano as well. She looks as though she might sit and play,
but then she gets up, puts on her coat, and leaves. The
lights shift to ELAINE.

ELAINE

(*to the audience*) Each little piece is a story. (*sitting at the piano and playing throughout the monologue to illustrate what she is describing*) It's a little adventure. And mainly the adventure is about leaving home (*playing a simple arpeggiated chord up and then scaling down to the first note of the scale*) and coming back. You begin and you venture forth into all kinds of situations, key changes, modulations, time, and tempo – you explore and experience – and in the end, you return home. Sometimes resoundingly so with a final cadence. (*playing a cadence from V to I*) Sometimes in gentler, less certain ways, (*playing the chord progression I–IV–V–vi*) but nonetheless securing the fact that we (*playing chord IV*) are home (*playing chord I*). Until we get to the twentieth century, of course, when we abandon home and the tonic (*while speaking, playing the twelve-tone scale*) and wander around in twelve-tone and Chance… the crisis of the twentieth century: uncertainty, new music, far from home, transient, mocking those who desire tonality, the familiar. Things change. They must.

> *The lights rise on* **TOM**, *who is hanging a sheet of opaque plastic over the window.* **ERIN** *enters her home and heads up the stairs, still in her coat.*

ERIN

Man, it's cold.

TOM

Yes. Sorry. I turned the heat way down so you wouldn't be heating the backyard. I'm working as fast as I can.

ERIN

No, no, I don't mean anything by it. I know it can't be helped.

> **TOM** *stops and looks at* **ERIN** *from the ladder, then climbs down.*

53

TOM
Well, I'm done for the day, but the good news is that the window is in.

ERIN
Can I see it?

TOM
It's not finished. I still have to do the wall and the sill.

ERIN
That's okay. I don't mind.

TOM
I know, I just... I don't want you to see it until it's all done.

ERIN
Okay.

TOM
It's just better to see it finished.

ERIN
I understand. I think perhaps you're a bit of a perfectionist, Tom.

TOM
Maybe.

ERIN
Well, I'll respect your artistry. I can wait.

TOM
Thank you. (*pause*) I've got a bit more cleanup to do here, then I'll be off.

ERIN
Okay. (*heading down the stairs, then pausing*) Tom?

TOM
Yes?

ERIN
I wonder ... I ... Would you like a cup of tea?

TOM
Oh. Yes. I would, thank you.

ERIN
Okay. Good.

> *ERIN goes downstairs, looking over her shoulder once.*
> *TOM picks up where he left off, waits until she's gone,*
> *then looks back at where she just was. Downstairs,*
> *ERIN hangs up her coat, grabs her own sweater, and*
> *heads into the kitchen. The lights shift to ELAINE.*

ELAINE
(*to the audience*) Music is an example of flow – of sound and
silence in motion. The interplay of two opposites ... one needs
the other. Music has to breathe. It has to have space and ... time.
Playing music is a relationship like any other. Sometimes it gets too
intense and needs some time to breathe ...

> *ERIN stands near the piano at ELAINE's house. She*
> *leans closer to look at the piece of sheet music that's*
> *sitting, ready to play. It is the Johann Sebastian Bach's*
> *Siciliano, second movement from his Flute Sonata*
> *in E-flat Major, BWV 1031, arranged for piano by*
> *Wilhelm Kempff.*

ERIN
Siciliano. I played that.

ELAINE
Yes. I expect you did.

ERIN
How old was I?

ELAINE
You were probably about five.

ERIN
I loved that piece.

ELAINE
It's a beauty. I've got two little girls, sisters, who I think would like it. I've arranged it as a duet for them.

ERIN
What a great idea.

ELAINE
I've been working on it all week. I think it's ready for them, but I won't have a chance to hear it before they play it. My plan is to give the primo part to the little one – just the melody – and the older girl, Elizabeth, will play the secondo.

ERIN
Right.

ELAINE
I've made the primo very easy, and I'm a little worried it may sound a bit thin...

ERIN
Well, let's try it.

ELAINE sits at the piano and looks up at ERIN, who remains standing behind the bench.

ELAINE
Oh, okay.

ERIN
Go ahead.

ELAINE starts to play the intro. Then ERIN stands, leans over the bench, and plays the first statement of the melody with left and right hands together, doubling the octave.

ERIN stops and stands abruptly upright.

ERIN
I think it's a little thin. (*sitting beside ELAINE*) How about this?

ERIN begins to play the same melody with an Alberti bass. She stops playing at the same point.

ERIN
Do you think she could do this?

ERIN plays the melody and Alberti bass.

ELAINE
I think so.

ELAINE and ERIN start to play together using Erin's idea – they play a bar or two. Then, ERIN stops; ELAINE stops as well.

ERIN
It's too much. She could just play the chord.

ERIN plays a G-minor triad.

ELAINE
That would work too.

ERIN
(*adding the melody to the G-minor triad*) Better, I think.

ELAINE
I agree.

ERIN and ELAINE both play a moment longer. ERIN stands, suddenly aware that she's been playing. She goes to the sliding glass doors to look outside. ELAINE

does not move. ERIN stands still, just looking out the
window. Finally, she points to the backyard.

ERIN
Can I get out over there?

ELAINE
Yes.

ERIN
Okay. I have to go now.

ERIN leaves.

ELAINE
(*to the audience*) I sat and watched her go. God knows what was
touched in her, but whatever it was, I thought: that's the thing
she's holding on to, that's the thing that's pinning her down, and
all I could think of was Bartók and Copland. She wants earth and
space, and I thought: let her go. (*pause*) Something happened
to me watching her leave. I don't know what it was, but I felt
scared. It was like something in me was leaving with her, slipping
through my hands.

MUSIC CUE: Second movement (Andantino ed
   innocentemente) of Haydn's Piano Trio no. 45 in E-flat
   Major, Hob. XV:29, performed by the Beaux Arts Trio

ACT 2

MUSIC CUE: "My Buddy," by Walter Donaldson (music) and Gus Kahn (lyrics), performed by the Steve Kuhn Trio

While the music is playing, the lights come up slowly, streaming through the window onto the landing. TOM *and* ERIN *are sitting in front of the new window playing Scrabble. There are two wicker chairs with cushions and a small table between them. A second, smaller table stands beside* ERIN's *chair with a pot of tea and a cup and saucer on it.* TOM's *teacup is on the floor beside him. They are leaning in, looking at the board.*

TOM
Come on, Erin, it's not chess.

ERIN
I know, I don't have any letters.

TOM
You've got seven.

ERIN
I don't have any I can use.

TOM
Not one? Just look for a vowel, like an *O* or an *A*, and if you have a *T*, you can do something.

ERIN
That's cheating.

TOM
No, it's not.

ERIN

Well, it isn't very clever. Anyway, I don't have a *T*.

TOM

What have you got?

ERIN

Four *O*s, two *E*s, and an *I*.

TOM

Wow, that's a drag.

ERIN

Mr. Sympathy.

TOM

That's me. Listen. Don't think too hard, don't think about making points, just get through this turn.

ERIN

The simplicity. Just get through the turn. No big gains, no perfect answer.

TOM

A bit of a perfectionist, are we?

ERIN

We are. Absolutely.

TOM

My perfection is mainly about my work, not so much the rest of my life.

ERIN

And you can separate the two?

TOM

(*shrugging*) I try.

ERIN

Ah. There goes two of my *O*s. Three points.

TOM

Excellent. Now we can move on.

ERIN

(*reaching into the bag and pulling out two tiles*) Ha!

TOM

What did you get?

ERIN

I'm not telling you.

> *ERIN arranges the tiles in the holder.*

TOM

That's fine. I don't need to know.

> *TOM sorts his letters, then squints at the board.*

ERIN

You know, there's a lot of wisdom that comes out of you.

TOM

Scrabble wisdom, Erin.

ERIN

I'm sure it goes beyond Scrabble.

TOM

I don't know about that. I've certainly managed to make some pretty unwise decisions.

> *TOM plucks a few tiles from the holder.*

ERIN

Now that sounds interesting.

TOM

I wouldn't say so. Okay, here we go. (*laying his tiles on the board*) "Violin."

ERIN

"Violin?" You're kidding.

TOM

See? The *V* is on a double letter so that's eight points... (*looking at her*) Hey, where did you go?

ERIN

What?

TOM

You just went somewhere.

ERIN

Oh. I'm here. Sorry.

TOM

No need to be sorry.

ERIN

Sometimes I get these... I'm still getting used to my life.

TOM

How long has it been?

ERIN

Just over two years.

TOM

Well. That's not very long.

ERIN

No. (*pause*) Thank you, Tom. (*pause*) I think we ought to return to the game because this time, I know exactly where I'm putting these two new letters. (*setting the tiles on the board in triumph*) There. On the triple word.

TOM

Well done.

ERIN

Twenty-one points.

TOM

Very good. Unfortunately for you, those points will not help because (*arranging his final tiles on the board*) I am out.

> *TOM counts quietly. ERIN watches him, smiling. He looks up at her and smiles too.*

TOM

You did great.

ERIN

Yes, well, thank you. I think I'm going to need a lot more practice, but maybe one day.

TOM

One day? That sounds like we have a future. (*suddenly self-conscious*) I mean ... a Scrabble future.

ERIN

Right. That would be nice. A Scrabble future. (*sitting back and looking at the window with a smile*) It's perfect, Tom. The window's perfect. Thank you.

TOM

You're welcome. I'm glad you're happy with it.

ERIN

You did a beautiful job.

> *Beat.*

TOM

(*standing*) Well, maybe I should get going.

ERIN

Oh. Okay, I mean, of course, you must have things to do ...

TOM

No, I don't. I just meant –

ERIN

I'm sure you're busy.

TOM

No. I'm not. (*pause*) I actually have no plans for the rest of the day. This is my singular Sunday mission: Scrabble with Erin.

ERIN

Well, this is my Sunday mission too. Learning to play. (*beginning to put the game away*) Stay.

TOM

Okay. (*going to the window and looking out*) It's very quiet here, isn't it?

ERIN

Yes.

TOM

I like it. It's peaceful. My place has a fair amount of traffic noise.

ERIN

I would find that hard.

TOM

I'm not home much. I'm used to it, I guess. You know, Erin, I was thinking that if you really wanted to make some changes to your place, you could take this wall down and open the space up even more.

ERIN

Oh.

TOM

What's there? (*starting towards the hallway to the bedroom door*)

ERIN

Nothing. (*standing*) A bedroom.

TOM

Well, it might bring down the value of your place. You'd have one less bedroom, but on the other hand...

> As **TOM** *heads towards Terrence's bedroom,* **ERIN** *leaves the table and rushes to stop him. She hurries around him and blocks him from going any further.*

ERIN

No, Tom, please don't. The room, it's... it's not very tidy.

TOM

That's okay, Erin, I don't mind.

> *TOM tries to manoeuvre around her.*

ERIN

No, please.

TOM

Okay.

ERIN

Thank you. (*pointing to the window*) This is enough, what you've done. This is just perfect.

TOM

I'm just playing. I guess it's part of my work to keep imagining the next step.

> *ERIN gently takes* **TOM***'s arm and guides him back to the table in front of the window.*

ERIN

I know that, Tom. (*pause*) This was a big decision for me. (*starting to put the Scrabble pieces away again*) I think I will just let it settle.

TOM

Okay, good. (*watching ERIN*) What do you do for a living, Erin? If you don't mind me asking.

ERIN

I teach part-time.

TOM

Kids?

ERIN

No. Adults.

TOM

Oh. What do you teach?

ERIN

Music.

TOM

Piano?

ERIN

No. History. I teach a basic music-history course.

TOM

You teach, but you don't play.

ERIN

Ironic, isn't it. (*pause*) How about I make us something to eat?

TOM

Sure, that sounds great.

> *ERIN leads TOM downstairs to the breakfast bar. She prepares lunch while they chat. TOM wanders over to the piano.*

TOM

Can you teach me to play?

ERIN

Do you have a piano?

TOM

No, but I could get one if I decided to learn. If I had a good teacher.

ERIN

Well. We'll see.

TOM

Would you play something?

ERIN

I'd rather not. It's been a while. I'm pretty rusty.

TOM

I don't care if you're rusty.

ERIN

I do. Tell me about you. Where did you acquire this love of old music?

TOM

My granddad.

ERIN

(*preparing a simple meal*) Oh?

TOM

He took care of me growing up.

ERIN

Really.

TOM

Mom worked. Granddad was a builder. He had his own little construction company. He used to take me with him to the site when I was a kid. He had a trailer for an office. Sometimes I'd drive around with him to pick stuff up. No matter where he was, he'd have one of those oldies stations on.

ERIN

No grandmother?

TOM

Not on my mom's side. My dad's, but we never saw that side of the family.

ERIN

And your dad?

TOM

Bit of a drinker. Mom left him. Or maybe he left us, I don't remember. I was very young.

ERIN

(*pause*) So you learned how to build.

TOM

My grandfather could make anything. He could build a house from the foundation to the finishing. Taught me to do the same.

ERIN

Wow. That sounds... lovely.

TOM

I have vivid memories of him picking me up from school. One in particular – I was about nine – I was getting in the truck, and he had the radio on and he was singing along to it.

> ***TOM*** *sings a few lines from Gene Austin's 1927 song "My Blue Heaven," composed by Walter Donaldson with lyrics by George A. Whiting: "When whippoorwills call..."*

ERIN

You can sing.

TOM

Thank you. I'd never heard him sing before. I can still hear his voice. It was so clear. I thought: he's as good as anyone on the radio. And I remember feeling so proud that he could sing like that. (*pause*) Anyway. I was making a living doing small jobs by the time I was fifteen.

ERIN

Did you finish school?

TOM

God, yes. My mother would have killed me. I went to college, too. But doing this makes me happy.

ERIN

Why didn't you learn to play an instrument?

TOM

I don't know. Playing music wasn't part of the family. It was always around, though. I don't think I could live without it, but playing it? Learning music? Just never happened, you know?

ERIN

Yes.

TOM

You're very blessed to have the talent to play.

ERIN

To have been given an opportunity to learn. Yes. I am.

TOM

Makes you thinks, doesn't it? I mean, someone becomes a musician because they have the talent and the opportunity. Someone else with the same talent doesn't because the opportunity isn't there.

ERIN

Doesn't seem right or fair, does it?

71

TOM

No, but I guess that's life, isn't it? (*pause*) I think you just have to be grateful for what you do have and try to do the things you love.

ERIN

Yes, but sometimes it's hard. Sometimes it's hard to be grateful and to do the things you love.

MUSIC CUE: Third song ("Long Time Ago") in Copland's *Old American Songs*, Set 1, performed by Alan Marks

---

TOM exits. ERIN goes to ELAINE's house for a lesson.

ELAINE

Erin. Come on in.

ERIN

(*entering*) Hi.

ELAINE

I didn't know if I was going to see you today.

ERIN

I know. Me either.

> *The music cue fades. ERIN sits on the piano bench and faces the living room. There is manuscript paper on the bench beside her.*

ERIN

I'm sorry about the way I left the other day.

ELAINE

What happened?

ERIN

I just... I couldn't be here and then when I got to the street, I felt this anger rip through me. I felt tricked, betrayed...

ELAINE

Oh, Erin.

ERIN

By the time I got home I wasn't coming back for any more lessons.

ELAINE

But you did come back.

ERIN

Yes.

ELAINE

Erin, I would never trick you into playing.

ERIN

Then what *was* that?

ELAINE

You couldn't help yourself, Erin. You just did what you do... it was natural. It was your impulse.

ERIN

That's a trick.

ELAINE

Is it? I didn't mean it to be.

ERIN

Really.

ELAINE

Honestly, Erin, you're giving me too much credit.

ERIN

It wasn't intentional?

ELAINE

No. (*thinking*) Oh God, maybe it was a trick, but I certainly didn't mean it to be.

ERIN
Thank you. (*smiling at last*) So, what are you working on?

ERIN *gestures to the manuscript paper.*

ELAINE
Oh. (*picking up the sheets and setting them on the left side of the music stand*) It's for one of my students.

ERIN
Another duet?

ELAINE
Yes. So, how are you? How are the renovations going?

ERIN
They're done, the window's in.

ELAINE
And?

ERIN
And it's beautiful. The whole house feels different. It's like I have another room. I feel like I can breathe.

ELAINE
That's fantastic, Erin. I'm happy for you.

ERIN
It was your inspiration.

ELAINE
Right, well, you went with it.

ERIN
(*pause*) Tom came over and taught me to play Scrabble.

ELAINE
Did he?

ERIN
He's so easy to be around. Besides coming here, it was the most normal I've felt in ages.

ELAINE
That's wonderful.

ERIN
He asked me to a movie.

ELAINE
Are you going to go?

ERIN
I don't know. I told him I'm not ready or interested in any sort of dating situation.

ELAINE
Well, that's very proactive.

ERIN
I feel like I have a friend – someone new and nice and happy – who doesn't know anything about me or my life and... and (*growing sad*) I like how it feels.

ELAINE
Right. Well, that makes sense.

ERIN
I mean, he knows about Kevin, but I haven't told him anything else. I just... I don't want to go into the whole thing right now. I just want this to stay simple and uncomplicated.

ELAINE
You've only just met him, I'm sure the time will present itself.

ERIN
When I'm with Tom, I feel calm and like I'm here and I think I should tell him. I know I have to, and I want to, but every time I go to say something, every time I even think about Terre... I still...

(*pause*) Elaine, I can't even talk about Terrence. I haven't touched his room. Sometimes I look into it, but I don't go in. I don't know what to do, so I don't do anything.

ELAINE

I can't imagine.

ERIN

(*nodding*) Yeah.

ELAINE

I don't know what to say to you.

ERIN

It feels like I'm leaving them.

ELAINE

You're not leaving them, Erin. You've made a friend, that's all. It's good. It's good.

ERIN

I miss Kevin.

ELAINE

I know. (*sitting with* ERIN *a moment, then trying to lighten the mood*) Come on, let's play.

> ELAINE *reaches out to* ERIN *and brings her to the piano.* ERIN *sits at the piano and puts her hands on the keys. She does not play.* ELAINE *sits with her and starts to play the bass line that runs under the melody of Bach's Siciliano (second movement in G minor of Bach's Flute Sonata in E-flat Major, BWV 1031). She uses this baseline as an introduction until* ERIN *joins and plays the melody. They play the duet together until the key change from G minor to E-flat major. The music cue picks up at the exact place they stop playing.*

MUSIC CUE: Third movement (Allegro) of Bach's Flute
Sonata in E-flat Major, BWV 1031, arranged for piano
by Wilhelm Kempff

*ERIN gets up and goes home, heading upstairs to
the landing. She stands in the doorway of Terrence's
bedroom and peers in. The music continues to play.
ERIN steps into the dark bedroom. The lights fade on
ERIN. The music cue fades as ELAINE begins to speak.*

ELAINE
(*to the audience*) I thought of Erin looking into her son's room,
and I thought of my life and the rooms I would have filled with
music, all those empty rooms I don't go into either. Of course,
I didn't know what to say to her. (*pause*) I don't know how many
times we played that duet. I think for the next three or four lessons
anyway. I was elated, of course, truly elated. She wouldn't play
anything on her own, but she was playing and that was something.
The fact that it was the saddest sounding song in the world didn't
make me happy, but I wasn't going to complain, nor was I going to
stay with it. But timing is everything.

*ERIN knocks on ELAINE's door. ELAINE smiles. The
knock is an example of this "timing." ERIN enters with
flowers and hands them to ELAINE.*

ELAINE
What's this?

ERIN
Flowers. They're for you.

ELAINE
Why? What for?

ERIN
(*shrugging*) It's spring.

77

ELAINE finds a vase and sets the flowers in it as they talk in a light and familiar manner.

ELAINE

Oh, they're lovely. No one has bought me flowers in a while.

ERIN sits at the table, feeling at home and comfortable.

ERIN

Kevin used to buy me tulips every spring. I saw them today. I haven't noticed flowers till now. I think you have something to do with that.

ELAINE

Thank you, Erin, that's very sweet of you. (*setting the vase on the table*) So. You're good?

ERIN

I am.

ELAINE

Good, then have a look behind you.

ERIN turns to look at the piano. There is a music book on the bench.

ERIN

Schubert's Fantasia in F Minor. Oh my God, this duet! It's so beautiful.

ERIN goes to the piano, sits on the bench, and puts the music on the stand. ELAINE joins ERIN at the piano.

ELAINE

The melody is absolutely haunting.

ERIN

(*positioning herself to play*) I love when it gets restated in the major key.

*ERIN and ELAINE sit side by side looking at the
music. ELAINE rubs her hands slightly and puts them
on the keys.*

ELAINE
I know, it's like the sun coming out. (*pause*) I used to play this
duet. It's been years.

*ELAINE begins the bass pattern and ERIN joins with
the right-hand melody. They play until ELAINE hits a
wrong note and stops.*

ELAINE
Damn. Sorry.

ERIN
That's okay. Let's just start again.

ELAINE
From the top?

ERIN
Sure.

*They begin to play again. A moment later, ELAINE
starts to falter and hits the wrong note again. ERIN
plays over until ELAINE takes her hands off the keys
and folds them in her lap.*

ERIN
Elaine?

ELAINE
I can't. It's… oh, this is awful. (*rubbing her fingers, agitated*)
My fingers won't do what my brain is telling them to do. I don't
know what I was thinking. Erin, this is not… I feel humiliated.

ERIN
Oh, Elaine, no. Please don't. It's just me.

ELAINE
Right. It's just you. Perfect.

ERIN
Come on, Elaine. Play with me. We don't have to impress anyone.

ELAINE
That's good, because it's not going to happen.

> *ELAINE puts her hands back on the keys and plays*
> *slowly until the music cue takes over.*

MUSIC CUE: First movement (Allegro molto moderato)
of Schubert's Fantasia in F Minor, D. 940

> *They listen to the music together for a moment. The*
> *music fades slightly. ERIN returns home. While the*
> *music plays, we experience the passage of time. The*
> *music fades completely as ELAINE begins to speak.*

ELAINE
(*to the audience*) It's a workout. Once you get past those first few
bars, you have to be able, and I no longer am. Later we played
Ravel and parts of Debussy's *Petite Suite*, and little by little, her
hands started coming back. She still couldn't play at home, or sit
at the piano alone, but she was playing and coming back to life.

> *The lights go up on ERIN's home. TOM is sitting at*
> *ERIN's piano.*

TOM
Okay, I'm going to play you the only song I know.

> *TOM makes a fist and curls his knuckles over the*
> *keyboard's three consecutive black notes ($F^\#$–$G^\#$–$A^\#$).*
> *He plays the famous opening segment of "The Knuckle*
> *Song" a couple of times and looks over at her, smiling.*

TOM
You know it?

ERIN
I've heard it.

TOM
It's a duet. Do you know how to play it?

ERIN
I have to say I do not.

TOM
(*patting the bench beside him*) Have a seat.

ERIN
I... I can't.

TOM
Don't be stuck up.

ERIN
I am not stuck up.

TOM
Come on.

     ERIN tentatively sits on the bench beside him.

TOM
Come on, I won't bite. Here. You play this. (*showing her the part she is to play and then looking at her*) Got it?

ERIN
I think so.

TOM
Let's give it a whirl. Don't worry if you don't get it the first time. We can do it again.

TOM and ERIN play the duet together. ERIN laughs.
Then they both laugh and look at each other. TOM
kisses her. ERIN pulls away.

ERIN

Oh. No, Tom. I don't think I can.

TOM takes ERIN's hand and holds it in his. They look
down at their laced fingers. ERIN looks up at him and
leans into his shoulder. Eventually, they stand.

ELAINE

(*to the audience*) Music, like life, is a process. It's an accumulation
of time, knowledge, practice, and above all else, repetition. Hours
and hours spent working on the thing you love. Ten thousand
hours, the experts say, to become a master.

ELAINE sits at the piano. She rubs her hands and
begins to play Hoagy Carmichael's "Stardust." She plays
the first phrase, then stops and massages her fingers.
ERIN and TOM walk to another part of the stage while
ELAINE says the following lines:

ELAINE

Oscar Peterson had arthritis. From a very young age. It did not
stop him.

ELAINE puts her hands back on the piano and begins to play.

MUSIC CUE: "Stardust," by Hoagy Carmichael (music)
and Mitchell Parish (lyrics), performed by Lester Young
with the Oscar Peterson Trio

ERIN and TOM dance to the music. Once they part,
TOM exits. The lights fade. When the lights come up
next, ERIN and ELAINE are in ELAINE's home.
ELAINE is still at the piano and ERIN is standing

*nearby, in the same spot she and **TOM** had just*
been dancing.

ERIN
I wonder if my friends from my other life would understand why
I'd be with someone like Tom.

ELAINE
Meaning he's not a musician? He doesn't play with the symphony.

ERIN
I don't know if he's ever been to the symphony.

ELAINE
So take him.

ERIN
I don't care if he hasn't. I don't even know if I want the two worlds
to come together. (*pause*) He makes me laugh. I'm having fun.

ELAINE
So, let's see how this fun translates to getting you back into
the quintet and the recording studio and playing with the
symphony, right?

ERIN
Right. (*going to the piano and sitting on the bench next to
ELAINE*) Hey, do you know this?

ERIN plays the first notes of "The Knuckle Song."

ELAINE
Of course.

ERIN
Tom taught it to me. It's a duet.

ELAINE
You played that with Tom?

ERIN
Yes.

ELAINE
Where?

ERIN
My place.

ELAINE
On your piano?

ERIN
Yes.

ELAINE
Well. That's fantastic.

> *There's a mixture of happiness and disappointment on*
> *ELAINE's face. ERIN's breakthrough has happened*
> *without her.*

ERIN
I know.

ELAINE
Shall we tackle the Schubert, or do you think you'd like to take on Bartók? Are you ready to go it alone?

ERIN
No. I don't think I am ready to go it alone.

ELAINE
Fine. How about Debussy? I don't think I can face Schubert today.

ERIN
(*getting the music ready to play*) Can I ask you something?

ELAINE
Yes.

ERIN

How long have your hands been so...?

ELAINE

Useless?

ERIN

I was going to say something a little less...

ELAINE

Truthful?

ERIN

Harsh.

ELAINE

It's fine, Erin, I'm good. It's just the truth. These are my hands.

ERIN

I hadn't really noticed until the other day.

ELAINE

(*looking at her hands*) Yes, well, I'm a very adept faker.

ERIN

So, how long did it take for this... I mean how long has this been...

ELAINE

Quite a while, actually. It certainly didn't happen overnight.

ERIN

(*pause*) So, could you have made a career as a pianist?

ELAINE

I didn't see the point. I mean, I had this inevitable outcome hanging over me.

ERIN

I don't know how you coped.

ELAINE

I didn't. I lost it entirely. It took a long time, but when I came to my senses, I went back to school. I thought I could learn to improvise, arrange...

ERIN

So hard.

ELAINE

It was. Especially since it involves so much theory and I'd never really been interested in theory. I didn't get it. I didn't like it. I'd always just scraped by. Now I actually had to learn the stuff. I mean, I could feel and interpret, that's what I loved.

ERIN

Exactly.

ELAINE

So, of course, I ended up in a theory class where the average age was about twelve, including the instructor, I swear. And all male, for some reason.

ERIN

What is that about?

ELAINE

I don't know. I felt like a den mother. Then it turned into this incredible experience. Those young men knew everything there was to know about root movements, chord progressions, augmented fifths, and altered sevenths. Their knowledge was breathtaking. Most days, I felt like my head would explode, but here's the funny thing: they could read and analyze and do the theory, but they weren't players. I could play, but in that room, playing didn't matter, and that was good for me. It gave me a whole new way to be with music.

ERIN

So you stopped playing. Interpreting and feeling –

ELAINE

(*slightly agitated*) I don't know if I'd say that –

ERIN

And went into the intellectual. The theoretical.

> *ERIN hit a nerve. ELAINE struggles a bit to get
> back on track.*

ELAINE

Yes, I suppose, in a sense, though I think the truth is I expanded
my capacity. You get on with it, right? Which is what we should be
doing, getting on with your lesson.

ERIN

Yes.

> *The lights fade on ERIN and rise on ELAINE as she
> returns to her lecture.*

ELAINE

(*to the audience*) There's something that happens when you're
learning a new piece of music. (*standing from the piano and
moving slowly to the kitchen*) You sit down and read it and it
goes beautifully. But then the next time you go to play it, it all
falls apart. That's because the first time you see the piece, you are
completely present. By even the second time, you've even begun
to think you know it. You're trying to sound polished, which,
of course, doesn't work. In order to learn a piece, *really* learn it,
you have to pull it apart, make a ton of mistakes. You can't care
what it sounds like, because if you're always performing, trying
to make it sound perfect, you'll end up with nothing. You cannot
perform until you've completed the messy process of practising,
making mistakes, misunderstandings, assumptions, and all.

> *ELAINE goes to her kitchen. She bangs a toolbox on the
> counter and starts working on her sink. The lights go up*

on ERIN and TOM. They are napping on the couch.
The banging of the toolbox wakes ERIN.

ERIN
I'm late. I've got to get going.

TOM
Where?

ERIN
I have a lesson.

TOM
A lesson.

ERIN
Yes, I have piano lessons Saturday mornings.

TOM
Teaching?

ERIN
No, I'm taking the lesson.

TOM
Why didn't you tell me you take piano lessons?

ERIN
I don't know. It didn't occur to me.

TOM
Why not?

ERIN
I have no idea... I just didn't think of it.

TOM
I don't get it. I asked you if you played the piano, and you said you used to but not anymore.

ERIN

Right. (*slightly agitated and impatient*) I don't.

TOM

But you take piano lessons.

ERIN

(*flustered*) Yes. I do.

TOM

Don't you have to practise?

ERIN

No. Yes. No, look, Tom, I'm going to be late. I'll be back in a couple of hours. You can stay here if you like. (*leaving for the lesson*) I'll call you when I'm done.

> *ERIN enters ELAINE's home. No one is there.*
> *ELAINE stands up from behind the kitchen counter.*
> *She's in a shirt and jeans, or an outfit less formal than usual. She holds a wrench in her hand.*

ERIN

What are you doing?

ELAINE

I'm fixing my dripping tap.

ERIN

So now you're a plumber?

ELAINE

No. Now I'm nearly out of my fucking mind.

> *ELAINE puts the wrench into the toolbox and closes the lid.*

ERIN

Call a plumber.

ELAINE
It's not hard to change a washer.

ERIN
Who cares? Why are you doing this?

ELAINE
Because I want to, it's been bothering me, I had time. Anyway, it's done. I was just turning the water back on.

ERIN
Oh my God...

ELAINE
What?

ERIN
(*starting to laugh*) Nothing.

ELAINE
Tell me why you're laughing.

ERIN
I'm surprised, that's all.

ELAINE
You don't do things like this?

ERIN
No, I do not. Nor do I want to. But I am inspired, truly.

ELAINE
Well, I'm glad I'm an inspiration. God knows you've inspired me. So. Where do you want to start today?

ERIN
(*pause*) Are you angry?

ELAINE
No.

ERIN
You seem angry.

ELAINE
I'm not. (*pause*) I'm not... angry. I've just had a banner day. I had three students in a row: a six-year-old who has already made resistance into a fine art, followed by another student who can't or won't read, I'm not sure which, and then a third who is so anxious he won't practise so when he makes mistakes he can say, "I didn't practise." And now you. I'm tired. And I'm frustrated.

ERIN
Me?

ELAINE
Yes, you. You do realize you're late?

ERIN
Oh God, yes, I know. /* I'm so sorry, I –

ELAINE
And I don't care that you're late, but I do care why –

ERIN
I overslept –

ELAINE
Right, forty minutes late and no phone call? This is not like / you.

ERIN
I was going / to call.

ELAINE
And it wouldn't matter one way or another, it's just, you came to me for help, and we've worked very hard.

---

*   Slashes in dialogue indicate an instance of overlapping speech and mark the start of the next speaker's line.

ERIN
I know.

ELAINE
You said you wanted to get your hands back. You *can* get your hands back and, I'm sorry, but I can't be part of you not doing it because of some... some infatuation.

ELAINE strides to the sink and tries to refocus her growing anger into busy work. She washes her hands and flicks on the kettle.

ERIN
This is not Tom's fault.

ELAINE
I know. This is you. (*pause*) Look, you said you know how to play but you can't, which I completely understand because *I* can't play, Erin. I actually can't. And I will *never* be able to play the way I was born to play. I don't have a choice. *You* do.

ERIN
You're right.

ELAINE
To have what you have, the opportunities, the future. (*suddenly realizing she has lost control*) I'm sorry. I'm not myself.

ERIN
What's going on?

ELAINE
(*pause*) It's hard sometimes. It's hard, that's all. I'm not in your world anymore, if I ever really was, I don't even know. You come here and it's like... it's like seeing what I could have done.

ERIN
What you could have done? (*shaking her head*) Look what you do. Look what you've done for me.

ELAINE

Thank you, Erin. I appreciate what you're saying. I do.

ERIN

I mean, I don't think you realize what an amazing teacher you are.

ELAINE

(*pause*) Arthritis didn't stop Oscar Peterson.

ERIN

I don't understand.

ELAINE

I got the news and I panicked. I just stopped playing. I gave up. There were things I could have done, but I ran. And I ran because I felt like I was going to die.

> *ELAINE breaks emotionally. ERIN sits quietly, respectfully, neither interfering nor attempting to rescue ELAINE in any way, and allows her the time and space to come back on her own.*

ELAINE

I thought I was done with this.

ERIN

(*pause*) Should we try to do some work?

ELAINE

Right. Yes. I have something I want us to try.

> *ELAINE goes to the piano.*

ERIN

Oh? What is it?

ELAINE

I've made an arrangement of something for you. I think you might like it. (*shyly pointing to the music on the piano and watching ERIN look at it*) It's from Copland's *Rodeo*.

ERIN

The "Saturday Night Waltz." Thank you. (*sitting down at the piano*) Let's see...

> *Not taking her eyes from the music, ERIN puts her hands on the keys but does not play. ELAINE stands a bit to the side, her hands together, hesitant. ERIN looks up at her and smiles. She pats the bench beside her.*

ERIN

Let's try it.

> *ELAINE sits beside her. They begin to play.*

MUSIC CUE: Fourth section ("Saturday Night Waltz")
of Copland's *Rodeo*

> *The music takes over as ERIN leaves, covers her exit, and fades out as ELAINE begins to speak.*

> *ELAINE gets up from the piano and speaks to the audience.*

ELAINE

I can't imagine better proof of God than music. People are forever swooning about the birth of a baby. Why? It's a biological event, about on par with a seedling pushing through the dirt, which is arguably also proof of God, but let's face it – if you're going to go down that road, everything is. No. I'm talking about the invisible, the ephemeral, the miraculous. Music is miraculous. Symbols on a page, little dots on lines, that amount to this.

> *ELAINE picks up the remote from the couch and presses a button. The music cue begins.*

MUSIC CUE: Second movement (Andantino ed
    innocentemente) of Haydn's Piano Trio no. 45 in E-flat
    Major, Hob. XV:29, performed by the Beaux Arts Trio.
    This piece should be played at a louder volume than
    previous cues.

*ERIN enters her home, grocery bags in hand, and
pauses to listen. Her eyes widen. She drops the bags and
scrambles up the stairs.*

ERIN

Turn it off! Turn it off!

TOM

(*looking down from the landing*) What?

ERIN

Turn that music OFF!

TOM

(*turning off the music and holding a CD up*) This is you.

ERIN

I know.

TOM

You didn't tell me you were a concert pianist. No wonder you don't
need to practise. I mean, for God's sake.

ERIN

(*cutting him off*) Who do you think you are? What on earth makes
you think you have a right to go into my things?

TOM

It was sitting in the CD rack.

ERIN

Right. *My* CD rack. This is *my* home. These are *my* things,
not yours.

TOM

I know that. I didn't think it would be a problem…

ERIN

Well, it is.

TOM

I can see that. I'm sorry.

ERIN

You shouldn't go through other people's things.

TOM

I didn't / think.

ERIN

You shouldn't go through other people's things.

TOM

I didn't know / it would –

ERIN

You / shouldn't –

TOM

Yes, I understand. I'm sorry. (*pause*) Do you want me to go?

ERIN

I don't know. No.

> *ERIN returns to the groceries she'd dropped in the entrance and starts to gather the things that have fallen out of the bags. Then she carries the bags into the kitchen, leaving TOM on the stairs. He follows her into the kitchen.*

TOM

Will you tell me what that was about, or am I going to have to figure it out on my own?

> *ERIN unpacks the groceries onto the breakfast bar.*

ERIN

Pardon?

TOM

I'm asking you if you will tell me why you just went out of your mind over a relatively minor privacy issue.

ERN

I told you...

TOM

Please, Erin. It's a CD.

ERIN

Yes and it was / on my shelf.

TOM

I know, we just went through / that.

ERIN

It was at the back. It wasn't even near / the front.

TOM

Please, Erin. Let's not do / this.

ERIN

You had to look for it. You had to find it.

TOM

Yes, I had to find it. Yes, I was looking through your CDs. Who doesn't do that?

ERIN

Me. I don't do that.

TOM

This is you! This is you playing! (*brandishing the CD*) Why didn't you tell me?

ERIN

Because I've been –

TOM

What do you do? Oh, I'm a concert pianist.

ERIN

I'm not a concert pianist.

TOM

You were. You are. I asked you what you did, and you said you teach music history.

ERIN

I do teach.

TOM

You made it sound like continuing education.

ERIN

It is continuing education.

TOM

That's damn near a lie.

ERIN

Damn near, but not quite.

TOM

Why lie?

ERIN

Because.

TOM

Because?

ERIN

Can we please stop this? Please.

TOM

How long have we been seeing each other? How long have I been coming here?

ERIN
I...

TOM
I can tell you. Five months and three days. And in all that time,
I realize I know very little about you. I mean, I know you, but...

ERIN
Tom...

TOM
You know, it feels pretty awful not knowing basic things about you.

ERIN
You know –

TOM
And I haven't pressed because I know you've been through hell,
and you've made it so so so clear that you can't, won't, and don't
want to talk about anything really truly personal. You can't be
completely here / with me.

ERIN
That's not true. / I've told you a lot about myself.

TOM
But honest to God, / Erin.

ERIN
I'm a very private person. I always have been. I'm not /
comfortable.

TOM
Do you have any brothers or sisters?

ERIN
A sister.

TOM
Thank you.

ERIN

I don't talk about myself. I would think that might be considered a relief.

TOM

What about parents?

ERIN

Ottawa. Both alive. And anyway, I don't think I'm so interesting that I should sit and hold court. Who cares?

TOM

I care.

ERIN

And what about you?

TOM

This isn't about me, but this is what happens. Every time I ask about you, you answer with a question, turn it around, and I end up doing all the talking.

ERIN

And that's great. I like listening.

TOM

So do I. You don't talk about yourself because this relationship is not that important, I get it.

ERIN

That's not true, Tom.

TOM

(*pause*) Is that your husband playing on the CD? Is he playing violin?

ERIN

Yes.

TOM
Thank you. (*pause*).Your husband's name is Kevin?

ERIN
Yes.

TOM
And you had a son named Terrence.

ERIN
Yes.

> *Beat.*

TOM
I don't know who you are.

ERIN
Yes, you do.

> *TOM stays silent and looks at his feet.*

ERIN
I'm sorry, Tom.

TOM
I know. I know.

> *TOM puts on his coat to leave.*

ERIN
Where are you going?

> *The lights go up on ELAINE. The conversation now includes ELAINE and takes place in both ERIN's and ELAINE's homes at the same time.*

ELAINE
Have you ended it?

TOM
I'll be back in a bit.

ERIN
I don't know.

TOM
I'm just going to take care of some errands.

ERIN
Okay.

TOM
I'll call you later.

> *TOM bends over and kisses ERIN on the cheek. She reaches up and takes his hand as he's leaving and shakes it slightly. TOM leaves.*

ERIN
I told him about Terrence. Well, he asked. He knew.

ELAINE
I see.

ERIN
He was very hurt and very angry. (*pause*) He said some things that were hard to hear, but they were true.

> *ERIN walks to the piano.*

ELAINE
I'm sorry, Erin.

> *ERIN sits at the piano and begins playing a few notes, a piece we have not yet heard. It is one of the Copland pieces, but she doesn't play it in rhythm, so the sequence is not recognizable. ELAINE notices and continues as though nothing out of the ordinary is happening. ERIN stops playing and turns to ELAINE.*

ERIN
Do you think I'm stuck?

ELAINE

I think you're doing everything you can.

ERIN

I think I am too, but Tom is right. I'm not here all the time.

ELAINE

Letting go takes as long as it takes.

ERIN

I don't know what to do.

ELAINE

(*completely relaxed, all her walls down*) That's the problem with grief, isn't it? There's nothing you can do other than let it in and just keep going. (*pause*) My younger students always want to play the parts of the music they already know. They avoid the hard passages. But you don't become a better player by avoiding the difficult passages.

>   *Beat.*

ELAINE

How would you work through a difficult passage?

ERIN

One note at a time.

ELAINE

Gently and kindly.

>   *The lights shift. **ERIN** moves to the landing.*

ERIN

I wanted to hold on to them, Kevin and Terrence. They were still with me from that morning. I was afraid that if I talked about that day they would be gone.

>   ***TOM** enters and sits on the stairs above the landing.*
>   ***ELAINE** remains in her home. **ERIN**, **TOM**, and*

*ELAINE are all in separate spaces. ERIN speaks to
them both.*

ERIN

It was winter. We were going Christmas shopping. I was home.
Kevin was rehearsing, and Terence had gone with him. He loved
to watch his father rehearse. He loved the orchestra. He wanted to
be a conductor. It was very sweet. They were very sweet together.
My husband and son. Kevin called and said they'd be home
around three. I didn't think much about it. I was home, working
on the Copland. I remember going to the window at around
three. I didn't expect to see them really, I just ... he'd said they'd
be home around three, so I went to the window. I remember
looking out at the sky. It was one of those winter skies ... thin
white clouds, the sun trying to shine through. I put the kettle
on. I felt cold. At three thirty, I called Kevin, but he didn't answer.
I remember feeling irritated. His phone would be off for rehearsal.
I thought: of course, it's so like him not to turn his phone back
on. But it wasn't like him not to call if he was going to be late.
It was starting to get dark. I was worried. I called the hall. No one
answered. I thought: well, maybe they've stopped somewhere. The
stories were starting in my head. I didn't want to call anyone in
the orchestra yet, you know, I didn't want people to think I was
anxious ... can't let the boys go for the afternoon, it's Christmas for
God's sake, a time of festivities.

Finally, I called Kevin's best friend, Peter. He said they'd left right
after rehearsal, going straight home, they'd said. I remember
sitting down. My legs wouldn't hold me. I knew. I knew. I told
myself that I was overreacting, but I knew. The whole world went
still. Not a breath, not a sound, no rhythm anywhere. I sat and
waited because I didn't know what else to do. I sat in the dark and
at 7:53 p.m. the phone rang. A drunk driver had run the red light.
It was instant. Diver and passenger. Both. Father and son.

Everything stopped. My life stopped. I couldn't speak. I couldn't move. I could hardly breathe.

> *Beat.*

My life ended that day. But I didn't die. (*crying now*) Holding on to Kevin and Terrence has been breaking my heart, taking my life. (*pause*) Letting them go (*slowly realizing*) has given me my life back.

ELAINE
(*standing in the same spot as at the start of the play, completing her lecture*) Music played from the heart goes to the heart. If you play with your heart and with honesty, you can actually say something. (*pause*) I wasn't prepared for Erin – how could I be? She was the teacher.

> *ERIN, dressed for a concert, enters ELAINE's home.*

ERIN
Hello.

ELAINE
Erin. You look… you look beautiful.

ERIN
Thank you.

ELAINE
Off to work?

ERIN
Yes. (*smiling*) I just wanted to stop in and see you before I go. To thank you, to give you your ticket.

> *ERIN hands ELAINE a theatre ticket.*

ELAINE
Thank you, Erin. (*clutching the ticket in both hands and studying it like a photograph*) Well. (*nearing tears*) Well.

ERIN

You'll be sitting next to Tom.

ELAINE

Oh. He's coming?

ERIN

Yes. He said he wouldn't miss it.

ELAINE

That's good.

ERIN

I should go. I like to get there early. You know, be in the
space, warm up.

ELAINE

Of course.

ERIN

(*hopeful*) Okay. See you later.

ELAINE

You will. (*pause*) Erin?

ERIN

Yes?

ELAINE

Break a leg.

ERIN

Thanks.

> *The lights shift.* **ERIN** *exits.* **ELAINE** *watches her leave.*

ELAINE

(*turning to the audience*) I am a piano teacher. It's not what I
planned, not what I thought would happen with my life. I tell my
students music is a relationship. You give it your heart, you don't
hold back, you don't shut down. You practise and you play.

*The lights go up on ERIN playing. ELAINE closes her
eyes and listens.*

ELAINE

It comes through you. And you and the listener are transformed.

The lights fade.

THE END

Playback Music Cues

In order of appearance

ACT 1

ACT 2

Acknowledgments

I would like to acknowledge the many people who were so supportive and helpful through the creation of this play. I am enormously grateful to Rachel Ditor for her faith in the play and her incredible dramaturgical wisdom. Thank you, Bill Millerd, and everyone at the Arts Club Theatre Company. Thank you to the amazing team: the cast and crew, the director and the designers who brought this play and these characters to life. Thank you to Kevin, Charles, Vicki, and Kara at Talonbooks. Finally, I would like to thank my mom and dad as well as my family and friends, with special thanks to Chris Allan.

Photo: Chris Allan

DOROTHY DITTRICH is a playwright, musical director, sound designer, and composer. *The Piano Teacher* was an Arts Club Theatre Company Silver Commission and Production that went on to win the Jessie Richardson Award for Outstanding Original Script. Other plays include *The Dissociates, Lesser Demons, Two Part Invention*, and *If the Moon Falls*, a thirty-minute monologue commissioned by the Solo Creative. Her musical *When We Were Singing* has been produced across Canada, including at the National Arts Centre in Ottawa, and in the United States. It received a workshop in New York with the Royal Manitoba Theatre Centre. Dorothy's work has garnered a number of Jessie awards and nominations, including two Dora Mavor Moore nominations for *When We Were Singing*. She is the proud recipient of the Sydney J. Risk Award for Emerging Playwright. Dorothy continues to write and read *Tippi and Stan*, a comedy series set in Vancouver.